Flower Cards
to Make and Treasure

Judy Balchin, Ann Cox,
Barbara Gray,
Polly Pinder, Joanna Sheen
and Patricia Wing

Contents

Flower Cards

to ...sure

SEARCH PRESS

First published in Great Britain 2010

Search Press Limited
Wellwood, North Farm Road,
Tunbridge Wells, Kent TN2 3DR

Based on the following books in the Simple and Stunning
series published by Search Press:

Handmade Art Nouveau Cards by Judy Balchin, 2007
Handmade Oriental Cards by Polly Pinder, 2007
Handmade Clear Stamped Cards by Barbara Gray, 2008
Handmade Fairy Cards by Judy Balchin, 2008
Handmade Paper Pierced Cards by Patricia Wing, 2008
Handmade Victorian Cards by Joanna Sheen, 2008

and on *Handmade Silk Ribbon Greetings Cards*
by Ann Cox, 2005

ISBN: 978-1-84448-554-3

The stencils used in the Paper Pierced Cards section of this
book (pages 58–79) are by AVEC or Anna Griffin.

Suppliers

If you have difficulty in obtaining any of the materials and
equipment mentioned in this book, then please visit the Search
Press website for details of suppliers: www.searchpress.com

Alternatively visit the authors' websites or email them:
Ann Cox: www.anncoxsilkribbons.co.uk
Barbara Gray: www.claritystamp.co.uk
Joanna Sheen: www.joannasheen.com
Patricia Wing: sales@stokegallery.co.uk

Printed in Malaysia

Publisher's note

All the step-by-step photographs in this book feature the
authors demonstrating how to make handmade greetings
cards. No models have been used.

Materials

At the beginning of each project is a 'you will need' list so that you know exactly what to gather together before making the card. Below are some general guidelines for cardmaking materials, and some more specific advice on what you need for the cards in each section of the book.

Basic materials

You will need some materials that are common to most cardmaking, such as a **metal ruler**, **craft knife** and **cutting mat** for measuring and cutting card and paper. Some projects specify a **guillotine** – you can buy small ones for crafts – but you could use a craft knife and cutting mat instead. You will need ordinary **scissors**, and some of the projects require **embroidery scissors**, serrated **craft scissors**, curved **cuticle scissors**, **fine scissors** and **decoupage snips**. A pair of **compasses** is useful for drawing circles. The drawing implements required include a **pencil**, **coloured crayons**, **pastel pencils**, **felt-tip pens** and a **gold leafing pen**. You will need an ordinary **hole punch**, a smaller **2mm ($^1/_{16}$in) hole punch** and a variety of **craft punches** including a snowflake, a flower and a rosebud shape. Finally, **tweezers** are recommended for some intricate work.

Paper and card

Gathering together your card and paper can be half the fun of cardmaking. For the cards in this book, you will need ready-made **base cards** (sometimes called **card blanks**) in a variety of colours, as well as **ordinary card**, **holographic card** and **pearlescent card**. You will need white **cartridge paper**, various **background papers**, **pastel paper**, **pearlescent paper**, various **handmade papers**, patterned **Japanese paper**, **origami papers**, **watercolour paper**, **textured paper**, **synthetic spun paper**, **lace papers**, **calligraphy paper** and a variety of **quilling papers**. It is also useful to have **scrap paper** and **tracing paper**. Some of the projects require sheets of **acetate**.

Adhesives

These are essential for cardmaking, and most crafters have their own preferences. Some of the glues needed are **clear all-purpose glue**, **glue stick**, **strong, clear adhesive**, **PVA glue with a fine applicator**, **spray adhesive** and a **mask**, **clear silicone sealant** and **latex-based white glue**. You will also need **sticky tape**, **double-sided tape**, **low-tack sticky tape**, **masking tape**, **low-tack masking tape**, **double-sided sticky pads** (sometimes called **3D foam pads**) and **adhesive putty**.

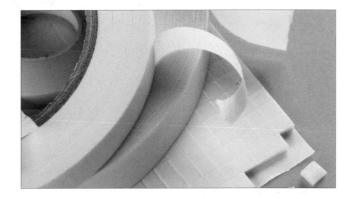

Rubber stamping equipment

The Golden Rose card in the Art Nouveau section requires a **Rose rubber stamp**, an **embossing pad**, **gold embossing powder** and a **heat tool**. The Victorian Lace card in the Clear Stamped section requires rose, Topaze and Victorian corner **clear stamps**, **large sticky yellow notes**, and a **dye-based eggplant inkpad**.

Embellishments

Cards can be decorated with all kinds of embellishments. The flower cards in this book feature **rosebud embellishments**, **fabric flowers**, **pressed flowers**, **buds** and **leaves**. There is also a **wooden heart embellishment**, various **gems** and **flat-backed pearls**, and a wide variety of **beads** including **tortoiseshell accent beads**, **ivory seed beads**, **leaf beads** and small **gold beads**. **Eyelets** are required for some cards, and these can be attached using a **hole punch**, **eyelet setter and mat**, or with a **Japanese screw punch**. Some cards are decorated with **wire** in various colours, and you will need **round-nosed pliers** to shape this and **cutting pliers** or **old scissors** to cut it. You will also need **gold-coloured head pins**, **gold brads**, **gold ribbon**, **glitter braid** and **glitter thread**, **cord** and a **paper doily**.

Special materials

As well as the general materials that are common to most cardmaking, you will need specific materials for some of the sections in this book.

Art Nouveau Cards and Fairy Cards

In both of these sections, Judy Balchin has used glass painting equipment. You will need black and gold glass painting outliners, glass paints in pink, yellow, olive green and blue, and clear glass painting medium for the Flower Maiden card in the Art Nouveau Cards section. For the Flower Fairy card in the Fairy Cards section, you will also need glass paints in red, light yellow, deep yellow and turquoise, and glass-painting gloss medium.

Paper Pierced Cards and Oriental Cards

Both of these sections require paper piercing equipment. For the Sweet Lavender card in the Paper Pierced Cards section you need a specific pricking template, an embossing stencil, an embossing and pricking stencil, a light box, embossing tool and a pricking tool and mat. You will also need a quilling tool. For the Flowers and Sparrows card in the Oriental Cards section, you will also need a specific brass stencil of a spray of flowers and a small make-up sponge.

Victorian Cards

In this section of the book, Joanna Sheen uses a design that can be printed out from a Victorian-themed CD of images. For the Dainty Doily card, you will need the Flower Basket image from the author's own CD.

Silk Ribbon Cards

Ann Cox showcases her silk ribbon embroidery techniques in the two cards in this section. To make the Single Rose card, you will need black linen, a knitting needle, a foam mat, glass headed pins and a mapping pin, various sizes of needle, various sizes and colours of silk ribbon, and toning stranded embroidery threads. The Fuchsias project also involves silk painting, so you will also need silk paints, paintbrushes, a tile, kitchen sponge and an iron, as well as white fabric and green coton à broder.

ART NOUVEAU CARDS

by Judy Balchin

My love affair with the Art Nouveau period has been going on for most of my adult life, so you can imagine my pleasure when I was asked to write this section, combining it with one of my favourite crafts – cardmaking.

The French term 'Art Nouveau' means 'New Art'. It was a wonderful art movement lasting from 1880 to 1915. This short period has left us with a legacy of beautiful artworks and designs which are still used today. The artists and craftsmen of this period used organic and ornamental shapes to produce flowing, intertwining work integrating all aspects of art and design. Simple or complex, the Art Nouveau style is instantly recognisable in its balance and harmony. It arose as a reaction to the Industrial Revolution, the high level of craftsmanship contrasting hugely with the machine-made, mass-produced goods typical of the day.

My biggest challenge in writing this section was to evoke the style and colour of the Art Nouveau period, and in particular the flower designs using paper, card and decorative embellishments.

I hope that you find inspiration from the techniques and ideas in this section. Use it as a launching pad for your own flower card creations and, most importantly, have fun!

Judy

Opposite
A selection of Art Nouveau greetings cards.

Rosebud Arch

Have some fun hunting down small, artificial flower embellishments to decorate your cards. Lilies and roses were used regularly in Art Nouveau arts and crafts. Soft, floral background paper and an arch of handmade paper are used to set off the delicate rosebuds. The wire stems of the rosebuds are curled to carry through the organic feel of the period.

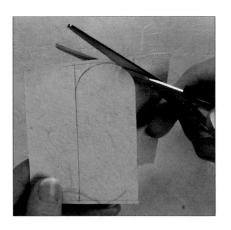

1 Glue the background paper to the base card.

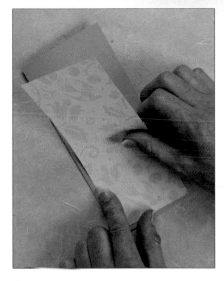

2 To create the lilac arch, draw a 4 x 9.5cm (1½ x 3¾in) rectangle on to lilac handmade paper. Use a pair of compasses to draw a semicircle at the top.

3 Cut out the arch shape.

YOU WILL NEED

Lilac base card folded to measure 9 x 20cm (3½ x 7¾in)

Lilac and blue background paper 8 x 19cm (3¼ x 7½in)

Lilac handmade paper

Pale blue card

Wooden heart embellishment painted pink

Three rosebud embellishments

Five lilac gems

Double-sided sticky pads

Spray adhesive

Pair of compasses

Pencil

Ruler

Round-nose pliers

Scissors

Scalpel

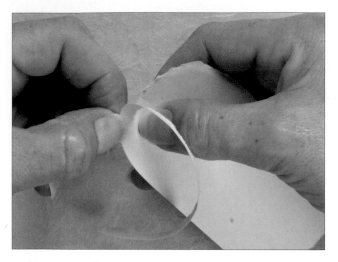

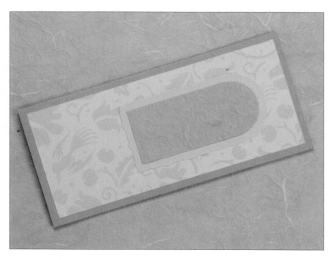

4 Draw another arch 6 x 11.5cm (2¼ x 4½in) on to pale blue card using the same technique and cut it out. Tear 0.5cm (¼in) from the edge of the card.

5 Glue the blue torn arch to the base card and the lilac arch on top.

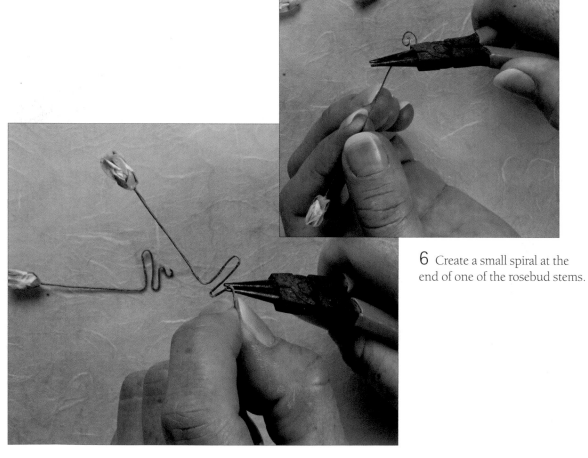

6 Create a small spiral at the end of one of the rosebud stems.

7 Bend graduating 'waves' into the ends of the other two rosebud stems.

8 Cut a sticky pad to fit across the heart embellishment and remove the backing paper.

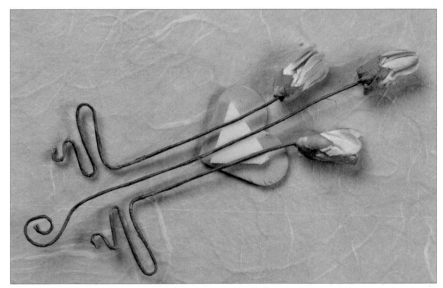

9 Lay the middle of the spiral-ended rosebud down the centre of the heart, and lay each of the remaining rosebuds on either side.

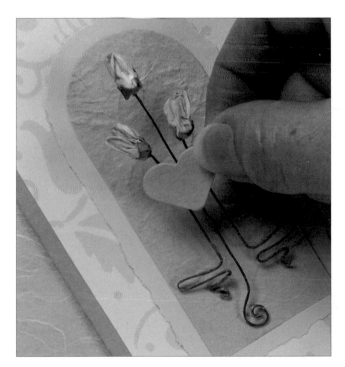

10 Press the heart on to the arch.

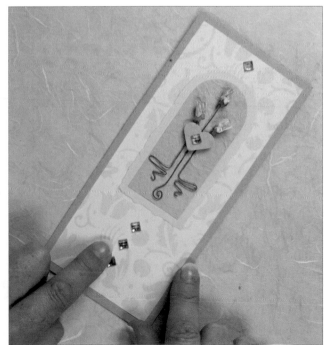

11 Decorate the heart with a gem, and glue three more gems below the arch and one above.

The antique key background paper in the card shown below left is used to link with the metal key embellishment. The stems of the lilies twine organically around the shank of the key to evoke the organic Art Nouveau style.

Foliage background paper and corrugated card are used in the card shown below right to back the delicate, intertwining lily embellishments. Simple jewels add a sophisticated touch. A matching gift tag is made using one lily. The lily stem is trimmed to fit the central panel.

A stamp-embossed border and textured handmade paper provide the perfect
background for the three lilies on the card shown above left. A small wooden heart
and a matching pink bow add a delicate flourish. One lily and a small ribbon bow are
used to create a matching gift tag.

The floral embellishment on the card shown above right is edged with a stamp-
embossed border. Deep colours are used along with the small punched dragonfly
and jewel to create a truly dramatic greetings card.

Flower Maiden

Stylised figures were used beautifully in Art Nouveau designs. Figures, their hair and robes, were flowing and balanced. This project shows you how to translate that harmony into a card using glass paints. Remember to apply the paint liberally to achieve a flat, glass-like appearance to your image.

1 Tear across the bottom of the background paper at an angle and glue to the top of the base card.

2 Tape the photocopied template to thick white card. Tape the acetate over the template.

3 Outline the design with black outliner. The line should be even and raised, leaving no gaps.

YOU WILL NEED

Gold base card folded to measure 8.5 x 18cm (3½ x 7in)

Acetate 8 x 16cm (3¼ x 6¼in)

Crackled cream background paper 7.5 x 12cm (3 x 4¾in)

Thin white card 8 x 16cm (3¼ x 6¼in)

Thick white card 10 x 18cm (4 x 7in) approx.

Template (see page 30)

Black and gold glass painting outliners

Glass paints in pink, yellow, olive green and blue, and paintbrush

Clear glass painting medium

Gold eyelet

Hole punch, eyelet setter and mat

Pink gem

Gold ribbon 25cm (9¾in)

Double-sided sticky pads

Masking tape

Spray adhesive

Small scissors

Ruler

Scalpel

4 When dry, remove the pattern. Create a flesh colour by mixing clear glass paint with a spot of yellow and pink glass paint. Paint the face.

5 Paint the hair sections with yellow paint diluted to different strengths with clear glass paint.

6 Paint the eyes blue and the leaves green.

7 Paint the lips pink. Fill in the flower petals with diluted pinks.

8 Fill in the border with pink paint and leave to dry.

9 Decorate the border with dots of gold outliner.

10 When dry, cut out the design.

11 Lay the acetate face down on scrap paper and spray it with spray glue. Press it on to thin white card.

12 Cut round the design and punch a hole in the top of the panel using the hole-punching attachment.

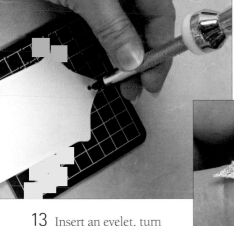

13 Insert an eyelet, turn the panel over and set the eyelet with the eyelet-setting attachment.

14 Thread the hole with ribbon and tie it in a bow.

15 Attach the panel to the base card with sticky pads and decorate with a gem.

The basic design for the card on the left is outlined in black on to acetate, painted and, when dry, decorated with gold outliner dots. It is then attached to the base card and decorated with gems. (The template is provided on page 31.)

The popular Art Nouveau butterfly design shown below is painted, cut out and mounted on to a base card decorated with floral background paper. Gems add a sparkle to the butterfly wings. (The template is provided on page 31.)

The tulip design above left is outlined and painted and, when dry, attached to a coloured base card. It is simple but effective. The matching gift tag is a smaller version of the card. (The templates are provided on page 30.)

The three panels of fruit on the card shown above right are outlined and painted. When dry, each is attached to a gold square of card and mounted on to foliage background paper. The panel is then attached to the base card. The matching gift tag uses a single glass-painted square. (The templates are provided on page 30.)

Golden Rose

I love stamp embossing! It is always exciting to see the embossing powders melt to create a solid image. In this project the central image is created with a rubber stamp, an embossing pad and gold embossing powder. To add subtle colour, the embossed image has been created on black card and then coloured in with pencil crayons. Backing the image with dramatic backing papers and embellishing with brads gives the whole card a rich, aged appearance.

1 Press the stamp on to an embossing pad and stamp on to black card.

2 Sprinkle the image with gold embossing powder.

YOU WILL NEED

Rose rubber stamp

Rust base card folded to measure 14cm (5½in) square

Rust card 6.5 x 7cm (2½ x 2¾in)

Black card

Rust-coloured patterned background paper 13cm (5in) square

Lettered background paper 7.5 x 8cm (3 x 3¼in)

Embossing pad

Gold embossing powder

Coloured crayons, red and green

Heat tool

Hole punch, hammer and cutting mat

Five gold brads

Strong clear adhesive

Ruler

Pencil

3 Shake off the excess embossing powder on to a piece of scrap card and pour the excess back into the pot.

4 Heat the image with a heat tool.

5 Colour in the rose with a red colouring pencil.

6 Colour the leaves in green.

7 Cut round the embossed image and glue to a piece of rust-coloured card.

8 Glue the patterned background paper to the base card.

9 Glue the lettered background paper panel on top.

10 Glue the embossed image to the centre.

11 Measure and mark five equally spaced points below the panel using a pencil.

12 Punch five holes through the pencil marks.

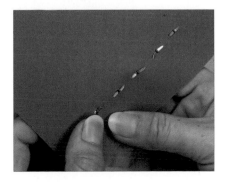

13 Insert a brad into each hole.

The central image on the card on the left is stamp embossed in copper and coloured with crayons. Butterflies punched from copper-coloured card and gold ribbons are used as embellishments to create a stylish Art Nouveau card.

The background paper on the card below is created by stamp embossing coloured leaves and small, gold dragonflies, forming the perfect background to this simple card. The tag is embellished with a dragonfly punched from gold card and tied with raffia. Make a matching gift tag by stamp embossing a single leaf and decorating with a single punched dragonfly.

Verdigris embossing powder and a small dragonfly stamp are used to decorate the crackled background paper in the card on the left. The central image is stamp embossed on to card and attached with coloured brads. A real shell adds the finishing touch.

A stylish Charles Rennie Mackintosh style stamp is used to create the central image on the card shown below right. It is then coloured with crayons, decorated with gems and cut out before mounting on to the backing card and papers. A matching gift tag is created using a smaller stamp and decorating with gems.

Templates

All the templates required to make the cards in this section are reproduced on these pages. You can also use them as a starting point for creating designs of your own. You may decide to vary the scale, using a photocopier, or to apply a different technique to create a card that is unique and personal.

Tulip design card and matching gift tag, page 23. These templates are half the actual size. Enlarge them 200 per cent on a photocopier

Flower Maiden card and matching gift tag, page 18. These templates are half the actual size. Enlarge them 200 per cent on a photocopier.

Fruit design card and matching gift tag, page 23, shown full size.

Maiden with hearts design, page 22, shown full size.

Butterfly design, page 22, shown full size.

ORIENTAL CARDS

by Polly Pinder

The word 'oriental' conjures up so many wonderful images, from the simplicity of formal, understated Japanese designs to the opulence of intricate Chinese brocades. The characters of Far Eastern alphabets are in themselves miniature works of art – they can create exquisite emblems without the addition of any other mark, and can form an intrinsic part of a painting.

Designing and making greetings cards is, in my opinion, equal to making a painting or any other form of high art work. The same creative process is used – the initial excitement when an idea develops into a distinct possibility; then the actual making of the card, bringing all the different components together to form a single image; the wonderful satisfaction of completion, and finally (and this is something not often experienced in the making of a work of art) the grateful appreciation and effusive compliments from the recipient – we hope!

To any committed students of oriental languages: I have done my best to write the characters as accurately as possible and hope that the meaning is correct, but please accept my apologies if I have made conspicuous blunders. Thank you.

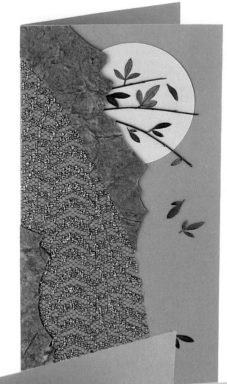

Plum Blossom

There is such a wonderful variety of pretty beads available now that it is often difficult to choose the appropriate ones to fit a particular design. Wire too has become an exciting material with which to work. I used to have to raid the tool box for little cards of fuse wire when I first started using it as an aspect of card making, but now it comes in different widths and glorious colours. When the two are combined – glittering, twinkling beads and twirling, twisting wire – a kind of magic is created in the finished card.

There are specialist shops where beads and all the associated materials can be bought, both online or mail order by telephone. They are also sold, though with limited variety, at many craft stores.

There are many variations on the plum blossom motif, and I have combined two to make this simple and effective card. Beads and wire are so versatile they can be guaranteed to enhance virtually any design. Here I have used four different coloured wires and twisted them to form the stigma, along with eight beaded head pins to represent the stamens.

YOU WILL NEED

Red card blank 13.5 x 13.5cm
(5¼ x 5¼in)

Plum-coloured paper or card
11.5 x 11.5cm (4½ x 4½in)

Craft scissors and curved
cuticle scissors

Striped pearlescent copper-coloured
card 15 x 15cm (6 x 6in)

Copper-coloured synthetic spun
paper 5 x 5cm (2 x 2in)

Red card or paper 5 x 5cm (2 x 2in)

A5 tracing paper and pencil

Eight gold-coloured head pins

A variety of small red, burnt orange
and copper-coloured beads

7.5cm (3in) lengths of pink, light red,
dark red and copper wire

Two cocktail sticks

Sticky tape, glue stick and clear
all-purpose glue

Small pliers and old scissors

Adhesive putty

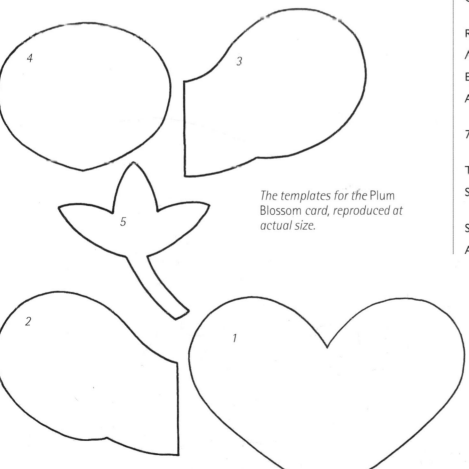

The templates for the Plum Blossom *card, reproduced at actual size.*

The template for the Plum Blossom *tag, reproduced at actual size.*

35

1 Using your craft scissors, cut the corners from the plum-coloured square. Stick it on the centre of the red card blank using the glue stick.

2 Transfer the blossom pieces 1, 2, 3 and 4 on to the pearlescent card. Using cuticle scissors, cut the pieces out. Stick pieces 2 and 3 together with sticky tape.

3 Glue the square of spun paper on to the pearlescent card using the glue stick. Press down firmly with some scrap paper and then leave it to dry.

Tip

If your pearlescent card is striped, make sure that the stripes are all going in different directions.

4 Transfer piece 5 on to the back of the spun paper and card, then cut it out. Transfer this piece on to the red card, cut it out and stick the two pieces together leaving a little red border at the top.

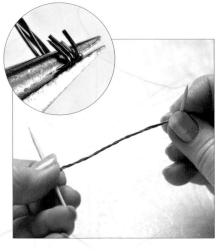

5 With the help of your pliers, hook each end of the coloured wires securely on to the cocktail sticks (see inset). Hold the wires and sticks firmly, then twist until you have a twisted strand.

6 With the help of your pliers, pull out and flatten the top loops of the twisted strand. Use your old scissors to trim off any excess so that the wire stigmas measure about 6cm (2½in). Press the stigma into the adhesive putty.

7 Thread the beads on to the eight head pins. You may find that tweezers help when picking up small beads.

8 Bend each head pin slightly and position them as shown, pressing them into the adhesive putty.

9 Squeeze some all-purpose glue on to the adhesive putty and then press pieces 2 and 3 on to it.

10 Stick the calyx on to the lower petal using the glue stick, then glue both of them on to the blossom.

The subdued background colours on this card act as a perfect foil for the striped pearlescent blossom and the sparkling stamens and calyx. Cuticle scissors made cutting the rounded petals much easier.

Tree by River

These little metal beads make perfect blossom. They are attached to the card with small pieces of double-sided tape. The tree (template on page 56) was cut from thick black cartridge paper, which then had pieces of the finest gold coloured wire wrapped around the trunk and branches.

Heron in Bulrushes

This was inspired by the well-known painting by Hiroshige, Bulrushes and Snowy Heron. *I have used straight pieces of wire to represent the bulrushes, a beautiful shark's tooth bead for the beak and a pearlescent flat bead for the eye. Everything is secured by double-sided tape. The Chinese symbol means 'happiness'. The templates are on page 56.*

Flowering Circle

This was inspired by a circle of blossom from my book, Traditional Japanese Designs. *Diminishing lengths of black wire were threaded on to some stalks and, using double-sided sticky tape, the blossoms and buds were attached to others. The little pink beads were threaded on to cotton and the black beads were pressed on to a circle of black card using double-sided sticky tape. The template is on page 56.*

Flowers and Sparrows

Piercing, sometimes called paper- or pin-pricking, is a new craft for me and I have just discovered how effective and wonderfully versatile it can be.

Since the mid-1700s paper-piercing has been used to embellish pictures and paintings, usually in the form of a decorative border and to replicate the delicacy of lace, but sometimes to accentuate fine details on the paintings themselves.

The tools needed to complete a design are available at most craft stores. The needles, all with integral handles, come in different shapes to produce a variety of pierced holes. The mat is dense foam rubber, which allows the needles to slide smoothly in and out. Both sides of the pierced paper can be used; the underside gives a raised pattern of dots.

Embossing is the perfect companion to piercing. Small brass stencils (as well as larger plastic ones) have a comprehensive array of designs which can be imaginatively used. Brass stencils can also act as guides for piercing. Embossing tools come in about four sizes; the smallest ball tip is used for the most intricate stencil.

You may wonder where the sparrows are on this design. The little images on the pink paper are the sparrows. You can just make out their tiny heads and outspread wings. If you can't find a small-patterned Japanese paper, you could use gift wrap or even wallpaper.

YOU WILL NEED

Dark green card blank 13 x 16.5cm (5 x 6½in)

Small patterned Japanese paper 8 x 16.5cm (3¼ x 6½in)

White cartridge paper 6 x 16.5cm (2½ x 6½in)

Fine black and red felt-tip pens

Light box

Tracing paper and pencil

Steel rule, cutting mat and craft knife

Brass stencil with spray of flowers approximately 5 x 7cm (2 x 2¾in)

Single piercing needle and piercing mat

Embossing tool with small ball tip

Pastel pencil (same colour as patterned paper)

Small make-up sponge

Low-tack sticky tape

Spray mount and mask

1 Lay the stencil on top of the tracing paper and draw the image using the black felt-tip pen. When the image is complete, move the stencil around and draw some extra leaves using the red pen.

2 Remove the stencil and use the red pen to draws some curved lines coming out of the flower spray. Put the tracing to one side.

3 Position your stencil on the top half of the white paper. Secure it with a piece of low-tack sticky tape.

4 Place both the stencil and the paper on to the light box, with the stencil face-down underneath. Carefully but firmly slide the embossing tool round the edges of each shape.

5 Remove the stencil and turn it over so that the image is reversed. Position it on the lower half of the paper. Turn the paper over on to the light box and emboss the image as before.

Tip

If the ball of your embossing tool does not slide easily on the paper, rub the tip on your hand or on some waxed paper. This should make it glide smoothly round the edges of your stencil.

6 Position the tracing accurately on top of the embossed image and secure it from behind with low-tack sticky tape. Use the piercing needle to prick along all the red lines, trying to achieve even spacing between each dot. Push the needle in as far as it will go to get the maximum size of hole.

7 Remove the tracing, turn it over and place it on top of the lower embossing. Secure it with low-tack tape. Pierce through the same holes as before to create a mirror image of the top embossing.

8 Carefully apply the pastel pencil to the base of each petal and bud.

9 Smudge upwards with the make-up sponge to soften the colouring.

10 Using the spray mount and mask, attach the patterned paper down the centre of the green card, then attach the embossed paper down the centre of the patterned paper.

This pretty card demonstrates how well the two crafts of embossing and piercing complement each other. On the patterned paper the sparrow images have been simplified in typical Japanese style, and reduced to tiny defined heads and rows of elongated dots which represent open wings.

Gracious Geisha

This lovely drawing was taken from my book, Traditional Japanese Designs. I have adapted her to fit the card and pierced the image using round and arrow-tipped tools. The hairpin embellishments are made from jewellery head pins, threaded with small beads which were then secured with sticky tape at the back. You can photocopy the drawing on page 57 and use it as a piercing template. The Chinese symbols mean 'woman' and 'beauty'.

Lovely Love

Heavy tracing paper was pierced with a heart-shaped piercing needle to produce the vertical strip on this card. I cut the stencil with waxed paper – the symbol means 'love'. See page 57 for the symbol template.

Beautiful Butterflies

I have used another small-patterned Japanese paper for this card, and a disc cut out using craft scissors to replicate the circles on the paper. I used a brass stencil to create the butterfly and pierced it to accentuate some of the detail. The little flowers were made using craft punches.

Formal Flowers

Origami is the Japanese word for paper folding and the art is closely connected to religious and cultural festivals, gift-giving and the craft of doll making. The production of paper was developed by the Chinese and adopted by the Japanese in 700AD. There are examples of paper folding dating back to 1000AD.

Origami is a simple concept but many of the designs are fiendishly complex and require great patience and dexterity. Here however, I have included little models that require only three or four folds in order to become recognisable. Even with such simple moves there is a great sense of achievement on completion – at least there was for me!

The thin but strong paper used for origami can now be found in many craft stores. There are packets of square sheets with different small-patterned papers, papers with a different colour on the reverse side and single-patterned papers in a multitude of bright colours. Wrapping paper, tissue paper and computer paper can all be used, and if the papers are thin enough, it is possible to glue them together to make a double-sided paper.

I have used double-sided origami papers to make the little flowers and stems in this project. The delicate Chinese pattern for the vase was originally on a surface-enamelled copper bottle. I scanned the pattern, changed the colours and then printed it; but any paper with a small ornate pattern will be fine.

YOU WILL NEED

Cream card blank 10 x 12cm
(4 x 4¾in)

Two strips of cream card 0.5 x 10cm
(¼ x 4in)

Two strips of cream card 0.5 x 20cm
(¼ x 7¾in)

Patterned paper 6 x 9cm
(2¼ x 3½in)

Two pieces of cardboard 4 x 7cm
(1½ x 2¾in)

Two double-sided origami papers
15cm (6in) square

Craft knife and cutting mat

Pencil and steel ruler

Double-sided tape and glue stick

1 Using the glue stick, position the cream strips 15mm (½in) from the edges of the card, laying one on top of the other at each corner.

2 Glue the two pieces of cardboard together. Use the pencil to mark, and then use the craft knife and steel ruler to cut along the two long sides so that they taper to 2cm (¾in) at the lower edge.

3 Lay the shape on the patterned paper and fold and stick the edges down with the glue stick, as though wrapping a present.

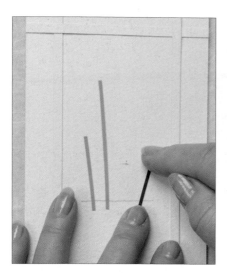

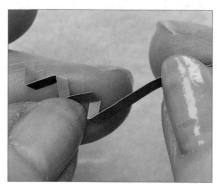

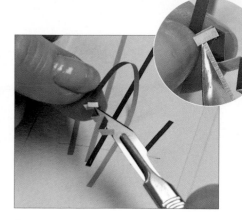

4 Draw a faint line just below half way down the card. Cut five narrow strips of double-sided paper – 4cm (1½in), 7cm (2¾in), 2.5cm (1in) and two 10cm (4in) long. With a dab of glue at both ends, position three strips, each attached slightly below the pencil line.

5 Make five concertina folds at the top of the two remaining strips, creasing first one way, then the other, as shown.

6 Position the two remaining strips on the card. Use a dab of glue at the bottom, and the tiniest sliver of double-sided sticky tape on one of the folds to secure the top. Use the craft knife to remove the backing from the sticky tape (inset).

Tip

Sometimes, if your paper is doubled, it is easier to initiate another fold by using a thin, straight-edged implement like a ruler. Position the ruler where the crease is to be made, lift the paper up and press it against the edge of the ruler, then remove the ruler and press down the paper to make the crease.

7 Cut two 4cm (1½in) squares from the double-sided paper. Fold the first square diagonally, point to point.

8 Open the square of paper up again and repeat with the other two points.

9 Fold the corners into the middle as shown.

10 Fold the corners out so that the two edges meet as shown, then make another flower in a different colour by starting on the other side of the paper. Make a third flower by following steps 7–10 with a different piece of double-sided paper.

11 Attach a piece of double-sided sticky tape to one side of the back of each flower (inset), then position them at an angle on the card.

12 Glue the vase and position it 6mm (¼in) above the bottom cream strip to finish.

These little origami flowers are created by only four folds of a square of paper. The paper is double-sided so that the inside colour of the flower is different from the outside. The ornate pattern on the vase complements the simplicity of the flowers and stems.

Pine and Blossom

Spirelli, from the word spiral, describes the craft of winding a thread round a notched template. The results appear to be very intricate but the process is really easy; and with all the fabulous threads available and a little imagination it is possible to create stunning cards. The basic process is to choose a shape, cut small 'V's or slits (depending on the thickness of the thread) at regular intervals round the edge, attach a piece of thread to the back, then wind the thread round the front and back securing it in the small cuts.

Commercial templates can be bought and you may want to start with them, but it is possible to make your own – just remember that there always needs to be an even number of cuts.

This design was inspired by a line drawing from my book *Oriental Flower Designs*. Pine and blossom are recurring subjects in Japanese design and painting, and they complement each other perfectly in form and colour. The Chinese lettering in the corner simply means 'good wishes'.

YOU WILL NEED

Blank grey card 10 x 21cm (4 x 8¼in)

Pink and white card 10 x 10cm (4 x 4in)

Grey card 18cm (7in) square

Tracing paper and pencil

Midnight sparkle glitter glue

Green felt-tip pen

Hole punch

Snowflake and flower craft punches

Glitter braid and fine green glitter thread

Embossing tool

Sticky tape, double-sided sticky tape and double-sided sticky pads

Scissors, cuticle scissors and serrated craft scissors

Tweezers, craft knife and cutting mat

Compasses or circle templates

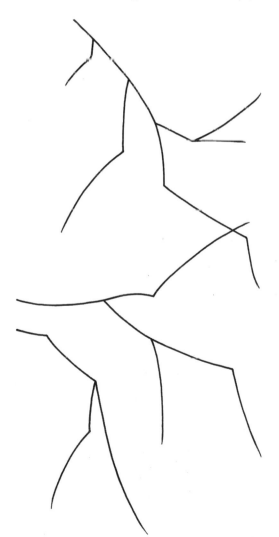

The template for the Pine and Blossom card, reproduced at three-quarters of actual size. You will need to photocopy this template at 133 per cent for the correct size.

Tip

If you have not used glitter glue before, practise a few lines first, keeping the nozzle slightly above the card, then lowering it and pulling away quickly at the end of each branch. An elastic band around the glitter glue tube and the attached nozzle will keep the nozzle cover out of the way while you are piping.

1 Draw the branches on to the card with a pencil and then start piping with the glitter glue. Leave for a few hours until the glue has dried and flattened.

2 Draw nine circles 17mm (⅜in) in diameter. Cut them out using your serrated craft scissors, making sure that there are an even number of notches on each.

3 Attach the green thread to the back of the circle using a small piece of sticky tape. Pull it over the front and round the back three times between two opposite notches, before moving clockwise one notch and repeating this action.

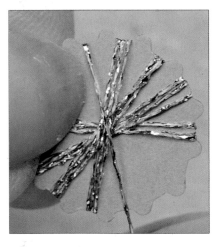

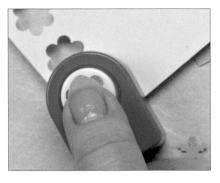

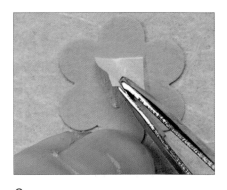

4 Continue working the thread clockwise all around the circle to make a pine symbol. Secure the thread at the back with sticky tape. Repeat this process with the remaining circles.

5 Punch seven pink and five white flowers using the flower craft punch; then seven white and five pink snowflakes using the snowflake craft punch; then, using the hole punch, seven white and seven pink circles, which will be buds.

6 Stick a square of double-sided sticky tape in the middle of a flower.

Tip
Tweezers make an excellent substitute for fingernails when working with tiny pieces.

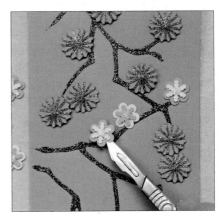

7 Put a piece of double-sided sticky tape on the back of a snowflake. Stick the glitter braid to it and wind it round the front and back of the flake spokes. This step is very fiddly, so use your tweezers: cut the braid and position the snowflake in the centre of the flower. Repeat with the remaining flowers.

8 Place a square of double-sided sticky tape on the back of each pine symbol, and position them as indicated on the diagram.

9 Place a square of double-sided sticky tape on the back of each flower and a tiny piece on each bud, and position them as shown below.

10 Transfer the Chinese letters on to a piece of grey card, then colour them with the green pen. Using the circle template and the embossing tool, emboss a circle round the letters. Carefully cut around the circle using the cuticle scissors (inset).

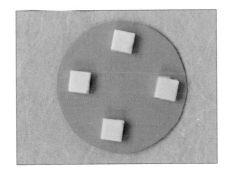

11 Attach four sticky pads to the back of the circle.

12 Position the circle on the bottom right of the card to finish.

There is nothing better for drawing these branches than glitter glue, which is a great invention and very versatile. There is a knack to using it successfully that will become clear very quickly with a little practice.

Falling Leaves

I have used beautiful handmade tissue papers for the autumnal colours on this card. I took the shape from the leaf stamp (used all over as a pattern on the left of the card) and made three spirelli templates wound with copper-coloured thread. The Chinese characters in the bottom right mean 'autumn'. The template is on page 57.

Sprinkled Cherry Blossom

These three blossoms were taken from a large print in which blossom images were tossed randomly to create an arrangement of negative and positive spaces. Here the arrangement is formal and the variegated silk thread produces a vibrant effect. The template is on page 57.

Goldfish in the Sea

This simple Japanese wave design called Waves from the Blue Ocean *was first used in the sixteenth century, then later as a decorative pattern on kimonos. I have cut some of the waves to accommodate the fish (template on page 57). These were secured at the back with sticky tape, and then the whole of the back of the card was covered with thin white card.*

Templates

All the templates required to make the cards in this section are reproduced full size on these pages.

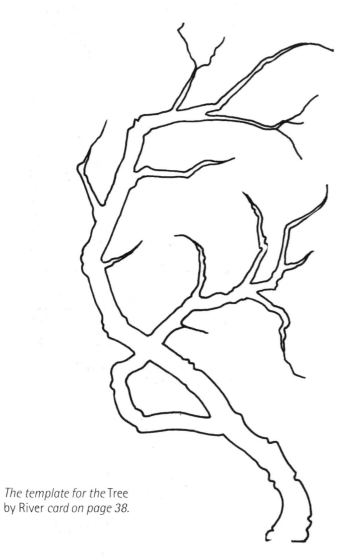

The templates for the Flowering Circle *card on page 39, right.*

The template for the Tree by River *card on page 38.*

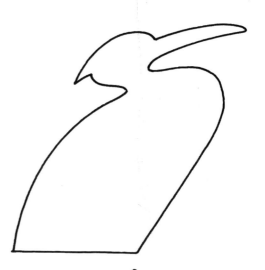

The templates for the Heron in Bulrushes *card on page 39, left.*

The template for the Lovely Love *card on page 44, right.*

女人美女

The template for the Gracious Geisha *card on page 44, left.*

The template for the Falling Leaves *card on page 54, top right.*

The template for the Sprinkled Cherry Blossom *card on page 54, bottom left.*

The template for the Goldfish in the Sea *card on page 55.*

PAPER PIERCED CARDS

by Patricia Wing

In this section you will find some of my favourite papercraft techniques, with paper piercing used to enhance the main design. I hope you will feel that all the different techniques work well together.

I have included the historic craft of quilling. This is quite a simple art to master, but I have seen the most exquisite designs exhibited. The Sweet Lavender card on page 60 has a quilled flower design with a pierced border, and it is finished off with embellishments.

Most cardmakers have probably used punches before. In the Rosebuds project on page 66, I show how you can achieve beautiful results using only one punch combined with paper piercing techniques.

Another historic craft included in this section is that of using pressed flowers. I have always enjoyed pressing flowers and of course this has been a delightful hobby for many generations, with flowers and leaves used to decorate bookmarks, cards, boxes and scrapbooks over the years.

Have a lovely time paper piercing and making the cards in this section.

Opposite
These cards illustrate the designs that can be created when combining paper piercing with other cardmaking techniques.

Sweet Lavender

Lavender is my favourite flower, and this quilled design makes a lovely card that someone special will want to keep. The petals, leaves and stems are made using simple quilling techniques. As well as quilling and paper piercing, the card features embossing and added beads and leaf beads.

1 Take the larger piece of ivory pastel paper and tape the pricking template to one corner using masking tape.

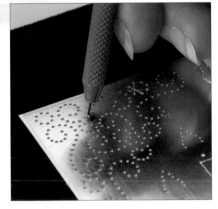

2 Place the paper and template on the pricking mat and pierce the corner design through the paper using the pricking tool.

3 Repeat for the other three corners. Mount the work with the pricked side uppermost on to violet pastel paper, using double-sided tape.

4 Trim a narrow border around the design using a craft knife and cutting mat. Mount it on to the folded card blank using double-sided tape.

YOU WILL NEED

Cream card blank, 142 x 180mm (5⁵/₈ x 7¹/₈in)

Two pieces of ivory pastel paper, 128 x 165mm (5 x 6½in) and 95 x 135mm (3¾ x 5³/₈in)

Pricking template FF 8032

Masking tape

Embossing stencil 5815 S

Light box

Two sheets of violet pastel paper

Ivory seed beads

Two leaf beads

Two 2mm (¹/₁₂in) pearls

Embossing tool

Pricking tool and mat

Craft knife and cutting mat

Metal ruler

Double-sided tape

Quilling tool

Quilling papers, 2mm (¹/₁₂in) and 3mm (¹/₈in) in various shades of green and lavender

PVA glue with fine applicator

Tweezers

Cocktail stick

5 Tape the embossing stencil on top of the smaller piece of ivory pastel paper on the light box and emboss the scalloped border.

6 Run the embossing tool round the outer edge of the stencil. This will create a frame around the design.

7 Mount the piece on violet pastel paper using double-sided tape and trim to create a narrow border.

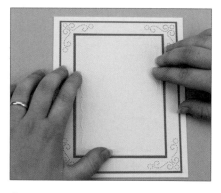

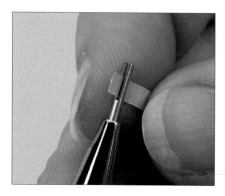

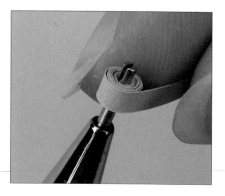

8 Mount this piece on the card blank using double-sided tape.

9 To make the petals, place one end of a lavender quilling paper strip into the top of the quilling tool.

10 Rotate the tool to wind up the paper strip.

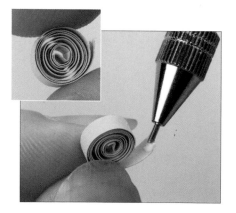

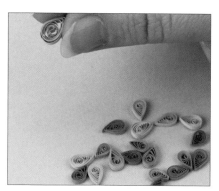

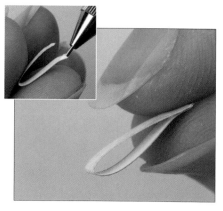

11 Remove the tool and let the coil bounce open slightly. Add a tiny drop of glue to the end to close the coil.

12 Form a teardrop from the coil by pinching one side. Make forty-five lavender teardrop-shaped petals; fifteen for each flower stem.

13 Form a leaf by making a small loop from a 2mm (1/12in) green strip and gluing the end to close it.

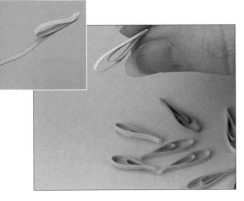

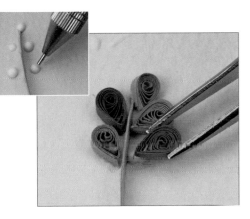

14 Glue a longer piece of the same strip to the first loop, bring the second strip round in a loop and glue to close. Make seventeen leaves in this way.

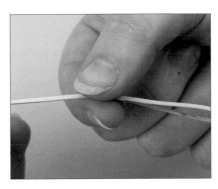

15 Glue and then pinch together two 3mm (1/8in) green quilling strips to make a double thickness stem.

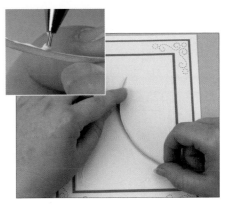

16 Cut a piece 110mm (4 3/8in) long and glue the edge of the strip to attach it to the card. Form and attach five stems, using the finished card on page 60 as a guide.

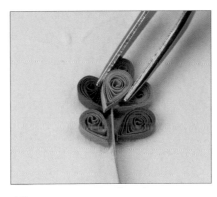

17 Place dots of glue where you want the petals to go, down both sides of the stems, and use tweezers to place the petals.

18 Place some petals on top of the stems as shown.

19 Glue on the leaves in the same way, using the finished card on page 60 as a guide.

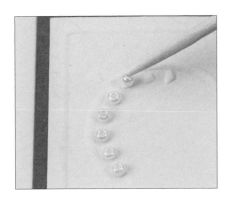

20 Glue ten ivory seed beads just inside each embossed corner.

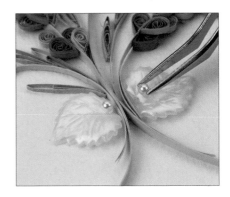

21 Glue on a plastic leaf bead either side of the stem.

22 Glue a pearl on each leaf bead to finish.

Quilled Posy

The pierced, lace-effect border from template Pro507 perfectly sets off this posy of quilled flowers.

Gorgeous Gift Tag

Here, the quilling follows the design from a rubber stamp, and this is enhanced by the pierced border on deep purple card (template Pm0550). Silk ribbons complete a gift tag that is almost a gift in itself.

Golden Butterfly

The gold butterfly on this card was made using a rubber stamp and embossing powder and it is enhanced by quilled petals made from parchment. The embossing on the cream central panel is from template FS948, while the blue pricked frame is from template no. 4.050.338.

Peach Dream

The centrepiece of this card is a gold metal embellishment (no. 4.054.118). The teardrop petals slot in to create the effect of a flower.

Rosebuds

Paper piercing creates a traditional setting for this contemporary rosebud design punched into three panels. Cool pastel colours, silk ribbon and flat-backed pearls complete a delicate and elegant looking card. All the items on pages 70–71 have been created using the same punch. Different styles can be achieved by punching in borders or on the corners, or by using different colours behind the punched rosebuds.

1 Using masking tape, stick the pricking template to a piece of ivory pastel paper. Pierce the design using a pricking tool and mat.

2 Draw round the outside of the template with a pencil.

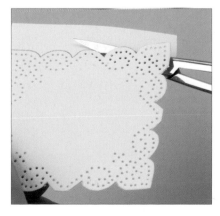

3 Cut round the pencil line with fine scissors.

YOU WILL NEED

Folded ivory card blank, 70 x 200mm (2³⁄₄ x 7⁷⁄₈in)

Three squares of lilac pastel paper, 58 x 58mm (2¹⁄₄ x 2¹⁄₄in)

Ivory pastel paper, 9 x 9cm (3¹⁄₂ x 3¹⁄₂in)

Two squares of mint green pastel paper, 9 x 9cm (3¹⁄₂ x 3¹⁄₂in)

Lilac pearlescent paper

Mint green pearlescent paper

Mint green silk ribbon, 7mm (¹⁄₄in)

Two 6mm (¹⁄₄in) flat-backed pearls

Masking tape

Fine scissors

Pricking tool and mat

PVA glue with fine applicator

Rosebud punch

Pricking template 4.054.118

Pencil

Tweezers

Double-sided tape

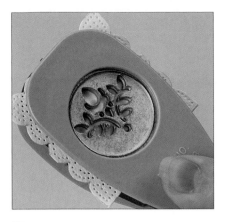

4 Repeat steps 1–3 twice more on mint green pastel paper.

5 Using the punch upside down, punch a rosebud in the middle of each pricked square.

6 Apply PVA glue to the back (the smooth side) of the ivory panel, around the rosebud design.

Tip

Use PVA glue instead of double-sided tape to stick down pricked pieces as it dries clear and will not show through the holes.

7 Cut a piece of lilac pearlescent paper large enough to cover the flower part of the rosebud design and use tweezers to secure it over the flower holes.

8 Cover the leaf-shaped holes in the same way with mint green pearlescent paper.

9 Repeat steps 6, 7 and 8 for the other two panels. Stick each panel on to a square of lilac pastel paper using PVA glue.

10 Stick the three panels on to the card blank using double-sided tape.

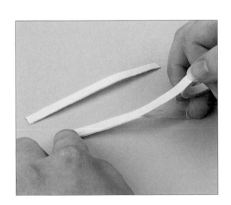

11 Stick double-sided tape to the back of the silk ribbon, peel off the backing and stick the ribbon between the panels on the card.

12 Trim the ends of the ribbon neatly at the edge of the card.

13 Glue a flat-backed pearl to the centre of each piece of ribbon.

Pearls and Rosebuds

The rosebud punch makes a striking design when used sideways on, and flat-backed pearls add a touch of elegance to the natural-looking colours.

Autumn Gift

Amber-coloured gems sparkle in this elegant gift tag in the colours of autumn. The pricking is from template no. 4.054.118.

Golden Roses
Lilac backing card works well with these golden rosebuds, and tiny gems set off the pierced central panel from template 10B 5A.

Rosebud Sparkle
This sumptuous card has been created using extra-fine glitter for the rosebuds and a tiny gold embellishment for the centre. The pricking is from template no. 4.050.332.

Perfect Pink
Handmade bookmarks make lovely gifts. Here the pierced design from template no. 4.054.118 perfectly complements the punched rosebuds.

Pressed Roses

Pressed flowers can be a reminder of precious moments in time. They vary a lot in colour but this helps to make each card you make with them unique. Use natural colours for background papers to complement the flowers. Accent beads stuck on to the centres of these roses really add something special to the flowers. Leaves and rosebuds have also been used to create a beautiful spray. A multipurpose pricking and embossing stencil has been used for this card and its edges have been used to create the scalloped central panel and the burgundy backing panel. Gems add a finishing sparkle.

YOU WILL NEED

Square ivory card blank,
144 x 144mm (5¾ x 5¾in)

Ivory pastel paper

Burgundy paper

Assorted pressed roses, buds and leaves

3D foam pads

Double-sided tape

Masking tape

PVA glue with fine applicator

Embossing and pricking stencil 500 000/5104

Twelve lilac 3mm (⅛in) gems

Twelve pink 2.5mm (⅛in) gems

Tortoiseshell accent beads

Fine scissors

Embossing tool

Pricking tool and mat

Light box

Pencil

Tweezers

1 Tape the stencil to a piece of ivory pastel paper and tape this to a light box. Using the embossing tool and working from the back, emboss the border scrolls round the edge of the stencil.

2 Turn the card over so the stencil is on top. Using a pricking tool and mat, pierce the small circles between the embossed scrolls. Also pierce the two central semi-circles.

3 Draw around the scalloped edge of the stencil with a pencil.

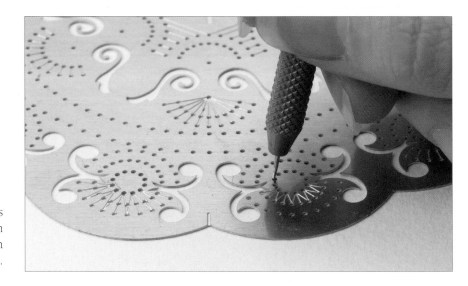

4 Flip the stencil over so that it covers the bottom of the paper, stick it down and emboss and prick the design again so that you have a circular pattern.

5 Draw round the edge of the stencil as before, then remove it and cut out the shape using fine scissors.

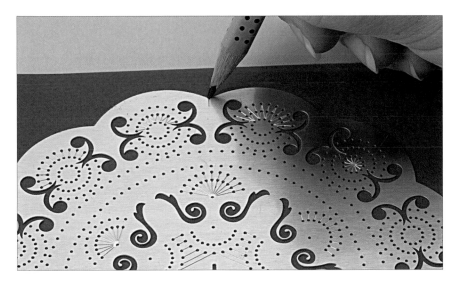

6 Stick the stencil to the burgundy paper and draw round it in two stages as before to make a scalloped circle.

7 Cut out the burgundy scalloped circle and mount it on to the card blank using double-sided tape.

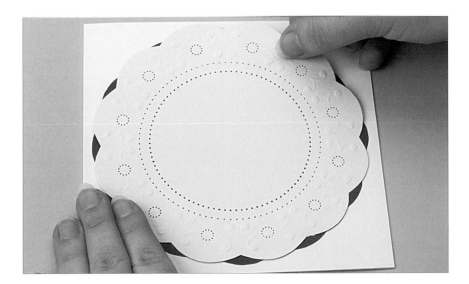

8 Mount the pricked and embossed piece on top of the burgundy scalloped circle so that the scallops show between each other. Use double-sided tape in the middle and PVA glue around the edge.

9 Choose four rose heads and put a large dab of glue in each centre.

10 Place the tiny accent beads in a dish. Use tweezers to dip each rose head in the beads so that the glued area is coated in them. Leave them to dry.

11 Referring to the picture of the finished card on page 72, stick on one rose with PVA glue and three with 3D foam pads. Use tweezers to help you.

12 Choose seven sprays of rose leaves and apply glue to the base of each stem.

13 Glue the sprays of leaves around the roses by poking the glued stems underneath the flower heads.

14 Glue two rosebuds at the top of the design, poking the stems under the leaf sprays.

15 Glue a 2.5mm (¹/₈in) pink gem inside each pricked circle.

16 Glue a 3mm (¹/₈in) lilac gem at the inner point of each scallop.

Naturally Perfect

Herb Robert leaves and hydrangea flowers sit beautifully inside an embossed frame and a pierced lacy edge from template Pro509.

Pink and Pearls

The swirling pierced pattern from template PM028 perfectly complements the pink larkspur and silvery leaves on the main card. Tiny pearl beads complete a very pretty picture.

Golden Butterfly

The elegant spikes of montbretia have retained their bright colour when pressed. The little butterfly embellishment gathers them together. The pricking is from an embossing stencil, LJ822, which can be pricked as well as embossed.

White Splendour

The yellow chrysanthemum with the beaded centre is surrounded by white splendour anemones mounted on green parchment with swags of piercing. The pierced corner design on the main card (template no. 4.050.35) completes a beautiful, fresh-looking card. The circle is from template Pro561.

CLEAR STAMPED CARDS

by Barbara Gray

The art of stamping is, I am told, the most popular and fastest-growing pastime in the world of crafting. During the past twenty years, it has evolved into a sophisticated art form, and using clear stamps opens up countless creative doors, because you can see right through to the surface you are stamping on to align the images perfectly.

Over the years that I have been designing clear stamps, I have developed many ways to use them, and this section will feature some of my tips and techniques which can only be performed with clear stamps.

You can spend a mint on accessories and supplies (if you haven't already!), but all you really need is a stamp, an inkpad, some paper and a quiet half-hour to start. When you first begin, I recommend that you just try playing with your stamp. Try not to judge your first work against the projects shown here: I spent many hours on them, and that was after fifteen years of practice! Just relax and enjoy the art. Skill comes with experience, but fun can be had along the way.

I hope that the projects motivate you to your own works of art, and when you have mastered the techniques in this section, why not borrow one of my recipes and add some spice of your own?

Remember, it is about the journey, not the destination. Good luck!

Victorian Lace

This card demonstrates the versatility of a little transparent corner stamp, which is used to create a repeating pattern and a seamless lace border. This sort of pattern-building is only possible with clear stamps.

1 Cut a 14 x 9 cm (5.5 x 3.5in) piece of watercolour paper. Ink up the rose stamp and stamp the image in the bottom left-hand corner.

2 Stamp the rose on to a sticky yellow note so the image is above the side with the adhesive.

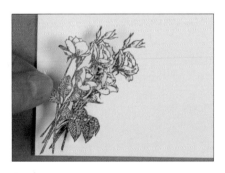

3 Use the embroidery scissors to cut the outline of the rose out of the sticky note, then apply it over the image on the watercolour paper as a mask.

4 Run strips of masking tape along each edge, covering approximately 1cm (½in) of the paper on each side.

5 Ink the Victorian corner stamp and blot it until it is a little faded, then stamp over the masking tape, allowing only the very tip of the stamp to print on the paper. Repeat this action to the left so that the second impression touches the first.

YOU WILL NEED

Clear stamps: rose, Topaze, Victorian corner

A4 sheets of 300gsm (140lb) cold-pressed watercolour paper

A4 sheet of lilac textured paper

Scrap paper

Dye-based eggplant inkpad

Low-tack masking tape

Five small gold beads

Lilac bead

10cm (4in) cord

Craft knife and cutting mat

Ruler

Embroidery scissors

Lilac colouring pencil

2mm (¹⁄₁₆in) hole punch

Gold leafing pen

Gold wire

Sticky foam pads

Large sticky yellow notes

Double-sided sticky tape

Tip
When pattern-building with corner stamps, always practise on scrap paper to get a feel for the little stamp before you begin.

6 Repeat all around the masking tape until you reach the start.

7 Run masking tape along the tips of the top border, then ink and blot the corner stamp. Stamp the tip into the spaces between the tips of the border.

8 Work along the row, stamping into each space, then remove the masking tape, being careful not to tear the rose mask.

9 Work around the other edges in the same way, then remove the masking tape and rose mask. Use a lilac colouring pencil to add a touch of colour to the rose.

10 Cut a 3¾ x 7½cm (1.5 x 3in) piece of watercolour paper, then trim the top corners off to make a tag (see inset). Ink the Topaze stamp and stamp the tag, then use the tip of the Victorian corner stamp to stamp a border as before.

11 Colour Topaze's clothing with the lilac colouring pencil, then attach the tag to lilac paper with double-sided tape.

12 Cut the tag out, leaving a thin border of lilac card. Punch a hole in the tag with the hole punch, thread the cord through the hole and then thread three beads (gold, lilac and gold) on to both ends of the cord.

13 Take a 5 x 12¾cm (2 x 5in) piece of watercolour paper and ink the corner stamp. Blot it and stamp the paper in the top right corner.

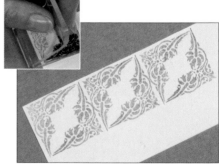

14 Turn the strip round, ink the stamp, blot it and stamp next to the previous impression, creating a square (see inset). Make two more squares adjacent to the first.

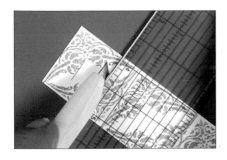

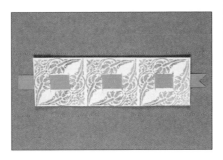

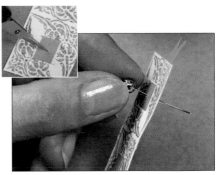

15 Use the craft knife to cut the motif out, then make a slit in the top and bottom part of the inside square of the designs as shown.

16 Cut a 0.75 x 14cm (¼ x 5½in) strip of lilac card and thread it through the slits. Make a swallow's-tail notch at one end.

17 Use the tip of your embroidery scissors to make a hole in the strip at the centre of each square (see inset). Thread a 7¾cm (3in) piece of gold wire with a bead, then poke both ends through the hole.

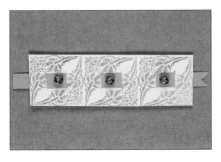

18 Twist the wire to secure the bead, and repeat the process on the other two holes.

19 Nuzzle the nib of the gold leafing pen on the edge of the motif and drag the pen along the side to edge it. Repeat the process on the main artwork.

20 Mount both pieces on lilac card (as in steps 11 and 12), then make a card from an A4 piece of watercolour paper and attach the pieces with double-sided sticky tape.

21 Attach the tag to the main artwork with sticky foam pads to complete the card.

Ornate Variations in Blue

This card illustrates several patterns using the same wonderful lace-making corner.

Three Honeysuckle Notelets

One small honeysuckle corner stamp; three delightful central motifs and a lovely border to link them to one another.

Catherine Wheel

Another variation using the Victorian corner. Here, the Catherine wheel actually rotates, turning on a brad.

VICTORIAN CARDS

by Joanna Sheen

My love for all things crafty has spanned my entire lifetime and is, I feel, the happiest hobby on earth. My specific interest is in looking back to times and standards of craftsmanship gone by. I love the gentleness of the Victorian era and the belief, so embodied in Victorian crafts, that 'if it's worth doing, it's worth doing well'. I see no point in making a card that looks as though you have not bothered to take care with your craft. I make quick cards all the time, but you should always take that extra moment or two to make sure you really are giving something that can be treasured.

I hope you will take inspiration from the projects in this section and will enjoy applying them to your card making. You can follow a card exactly and make a replica, or you can use papers or embellishments that you have in your workbox that will make your card unique.

The cards manufactured in those days had so many small touches of extra care – and I try to do likewise with my cards. Pretty inserts add a little something to a card. If you have scraps left, why not decorate the back of the card with a strip of toning paper and a craft sticker.

Many of the cards shown here feature toppers or backing papers printed out on a home inkjet printer from one of my Victorian-themed CDs. These are an invaluable source of images and ideas, but if you do not have a computer, there are lots of ready-printed decoupage sheets, backing papers and photographs available.

I hope you have many hours of fun both reading and using this section of the book and I hope you find the Victorian style as addictive as I do!

Joanna Sheen

Opposite
A selection of Victorian style greetings cards.

Dainty Doily

Victorian scraps are available already pre-cut, or you can print them out from a CD. Here a basket of flowers is very effectively showcased on a variety of lacy backgrounds from a ready-printed pad. The flower basket has been attached to the card with silicone glue, so it is nicely raised off the card to create extra interest.

You will need

Guillotine

Black and white, green and pink lace papers

Double-sided tape

Black card blank, 14.7 x 14.7cm (5¾ x 5¾in)

Paper doily

Silicone glue

Craft knife

Flower basket image

Decoupage snips

1 Cut all the lace papers to size using a guillotine: the black and white paper should be 13.8 x 13.8cm (5⅜ x 5⅜in); the green should be 11 x 11cm (4⅜ x 4⅜in); and the pink should be 10 x 10cm (4 x 4in).

2 Apply double-sided tape to the backs of the lace papers. Mount the black and white paper on the black card blank, and the green paper centrally on top.

3 Mount the pink lace paper diagonally in the centre of the card.

4 Apply silicone glue to the back of the paper doily, using a craft knife or a cocktail stick. If you use a craft knife, clean it straight away.

5 Cut out the flower basket image using decoupage snips.

6 Mount the paper doily on the card, then apply silicone glue to the flower basket image and mount this in the centre. Leave to dry for several hours, and preferably overnight, before sending.

D for Diana

*A decorated initial instantly personalises this card, and mixing the vintage image with
layers of lace and an organza bow is very effective.*

An Angel in Green

This beautiful child is decorated by circles of lace to echo the shape of the Victorian
scrap and then mounted on to layers of coordinating colours.

Pansy Duet

Pressed flowers lend themselves perfectly to card making as they are obviously completely flat and, when covered with acetate like this, they last for many years and make a treasured keepsake. In the language of flowers, pansies mean sentimental thoughts or 'thinking of you', and so they are ideal if you are making a card for a special person.

The lace and calligraphy papers used here came from ready-printed pads. You can of course choose your own to complement the pressed flowers.

YOU WILL NEED

Guillotine

One sheet of green lace paper

One sheet of calligraphy paper

Green card blank, 14.5 x 14.5cm (5¾ x 5¾in)

Double-sided tape

Pressed flowers

Latex-based white glue

Tweezers

One sheet of acetate

Japanese screw punch or eyelet punch and hammer

Cutting mat

Four gold-coloured brads

1 Use the guillotine to cut the papers to size. The green lace paper should be 11 x 11cm (4³/₈ x 4³/₈in); the larger calligraphy paper should be 13.5 x 13.5cm (5³/₈ x 5³/₈); and the smaller one should be 7.5 x 7.5cm (3 x 3in).

2 Apply double-sided tape to all the papers. Stick the larger calligraphy paper on to the green card blank.

3 Stick all the papers in place and use tweezers to place the pressed stalks and flowers.

4 Dip tweezers into some latex-based white glue (not PVA glue). Slide the tweezers under the pressed flowers and stalks to stick them down. Latex-based glue will dry clear so will not show. An alternative to using the tweezers is to slide a little glue on a cocktail stick under the flowers.

5 Cut the acetate to the same size as the larger of the pieces of calligraphy paper: 13.5 x 13.5cm (5³/₈ x 5³/₈). Place it over the card.

6 Open the card and place it on a cutting mat. Use the Japanese screw punch or an eyelet punch and hammer to make four holes through the acetate, papers and card front as shown.

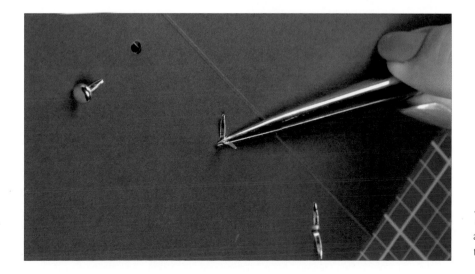

7 Push the brads through the holes and separate the backs using tweezers to secure them.

A Vase of Flowers

*This same idea can be used with many different shapes or papers to make the vase.
You could also stamp a vase, make a plain vase from card and decorate it with
craft stickers, or just use a suitable Victorian scrap.*

Roses and Metal Leaf

Here the backing paper has been decorated with flashes of gold and copper leaf, to add to the vintage, distressed effect of the card.

FAIRY CARDS

by Judy Balchin

I have literally been 'away with the fairies' while writing this section and have enjoyed every magical minute of it. The end of every day has found me covered in glitter and usually sporting a few gold and silver sequins as I wander round my local supermarket. This has naturally raised a few comments amongst my friends and family. So at last, here are my lovely fairy cards. The fairies have all faithfully promised to cast their tiny spells as you work. I hope that by the time you have finished making the cards in this section, you too will be away with the fairies... and proud of it! Have fun,

Judy

Opposite
A small selection of Fairy cards.

102

Flower Fairy

Create a little magic by using diluted glass paints to bring this vibrant Flower Fairy to life. Glass painting has always been my therapy, so get out those outliners and glass paints and enjoy the journey with me. She is backed with a starry sky of holographic card to give her that extra sparkle and sits delicately against a rainbow surround. Always apply glass paint generously.

You will need

White base card measuring
    11.5 x 19cm (4½ x 7½in) when
    folded in half

Thick card 14 x 21cm (5½ x 8¼in)

Rainbow background paper
    11.5 x 19cm (4½ x 7½in)

Silver star holographic card
    12 x 20cm (4¾ x 7¾in)

Acetate

Black outliner

Glass paints: red, light yellow, deep
    yellow, turquoise

Glass-painting gloss medium

Fabric flowers

Paintbrush

Palette

Masking tape

Spray glue

Scissors

Scalpel

Ruler

Crafter's glue

The templates for the Flower Fairy card and tag, reproduced at three-quarters of the actual size. You will need to photocopy each at 133 per cent for the correct size.

Opposite:
The butterfly template used on the tag complements the finished card beautifully.

1 Photocopy the template, cut round it using the scalpel and ruler, then tape it to a piece of thick card. Tape a slightly larger piece of acetate over the top.

Tip
Dilute each glass paint with gloss medium to give a more pastel appearance to the fairy.

2 Use the tube of outliner to outline the design. Leave to dry and remove the template.

3 Mix a drop of red and yellow glass paints with gloss medium in a palette to create a flesh tone. Paint the fairy's skin.

4 Paint the hair with diluted light yellow and the dress with diluted deep yellow.

5 Paint the wings with diluted red and yellow paints adding undiluted spots of red.

6 Fill in the branch, small flower and outer border with red glass paint.

7 Mix up a good quantity of diluted turquoise glass paint in a palette and fill in the background. Leave to dry.

8 Cut out the acetate fairy with scissors. Spray the back of the acetate with spray glue and press it on to silver holographic card. Cut it out with scissors (see inset).

9 Cover the front of the base card with rainbow background paper. Use spray glue to attach the fairy to the middle of the base card.

10 Decorate the fairy and the card with fabric flowers, attaching them with crafter's glue.

Flower Fairy can not wait to fly off and visit family and friends!

Fairy Queen

This glass-painted image is mounted on to starry holographic card. The cut-out image is then backed with a panel of glitter card. Small silver stars, gems and fabric flowers are used to bring this fairy to life. The matching gift tag uses a small glass-painted butterfly as its central image.

Toadstool Fairy

This delicate Toadstool Fairy is painted on to acetate and mounted on to mirror card. The cut-out image is then backed with a vibrant red card panel and holographic card. Small red floral gems are used to mirror the colour of the vibrant toadstool.

Love Fairy

Cards are made and sent with love. This Love Fairy card uses vibrant glass paints to send its cheery message. Sparkling paper and mirror card back the central image. For that extra twinkle small gems are used as embellishments. The butterfly gift tag uses the same basic coloured paints as the main card.

Templates

All of the templates on these pages are
reproduced at full size except where noted.

*Templates for the Fairy Queen card
and tag on page 108.*

Template for the Toadstool Fairy card on page 109.

Templates for the Love Fairy card and tag on page 109.

SILK RIBBON CARDS

by Ann Cox

In this section I have developed ideas and techniques from silk ribbon embroidery and simplified the methods of working to make them suitable for card making. The projects are small and therefore quick to work, so why spend hours searching for a card with that extra something when you can create one that is original and really personal?

First and foremost I am a silk ribbon embroidery designer and without doubt this is my first love. I only work with silk – its characteristics make it easy and quick for the embroiderer to shape each individual stitch. The only stitches I have worked for the cards in this section are ribbon stitch, straight stitch and gathering stitch in ribbon and straight stitch and French knots in thread, but I have used new and different techniques with them to create the flowers. The cards work on both fabric and card and you do not need to use an embroidery hoop. I also show you how to paint the ribbon, which increases the range of flowers that can be worked.

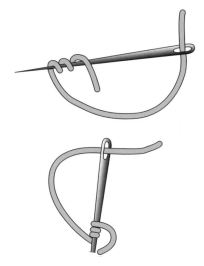

French knot

As you turn the pages of this section, I hope you will be tempted. There are new ideas and techniques to make card making easier and give a more professional finish. Use these ideas and never be afraid to experiment to create your own original cards.

Happy sewing!

Opposite
A selection of the beautiful cards that can be made by embroidering with silk ribbon without using an embroidery hoop.

Single Rose

This single rose, worked in 7mm (¼in) silk ribbon is a perfect project for your first silk ribbon card. It can be worked in any colour you choose, but using the two shades: pink (08) and pale pink (05) as I have here will bring the rose to life.

You will learn how to cut the card and secure fabric in the aperture so that no embroidery hoop is needed. I also show you a quick and easy way to anchor the ribbon (for card making only) and how, with care, to embroider perfect petals to create a rose. Finally there are the vital finer points such as the thorns and kinking the stem, the bow and assembling the card for that professional finish.

YOU WILL NEED

Two sheets of red card, 26 x 13cm (10¼ x 5in) and 12cm (4³⁄₄in) square

Black linen, 5 x 11cm (2 x 4¼in)

Craft knife, cutting mat, metal ruler and knitting needle

Glue stick

Plastic ruler and pencil

Foam mat

Glass-headed pins and a mapping pin

Needles: two size 18 (medium) chenille for ribbons, a crewel size 8 for embroidery threads

7mm (¼in) silk ribbon:

25cm (10in) each of pink (08), pale pink (05) and deep moss (72)

4mm (¹⁄₈in) silk ribbon:

25cm (10in) each of pale pink (05) and deep moss (72)

Toning stranded embroidery threads

Clear silicone sealant

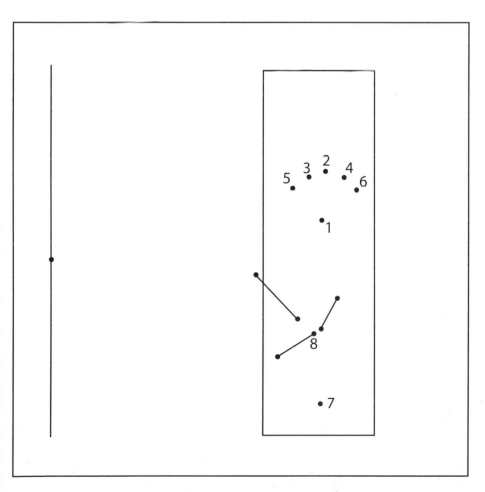

Tip

Always cut silk ribbon at an angle to prevent fraying and make threading a needle easier.

The pattern for the Single Rose card. Photocopy it to make a template.

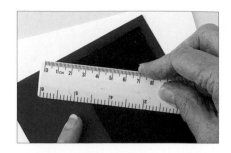

1 Use a metal ruler and a knitting needle to score and fold the red card in half. Measure and draw a 2.9 x 9.6cm (1⅛ x 3¾in) aperture in the single square of red card. Cut it out using a craft knife and cutting mat.

2 Reduce the width and length of the cutout panel by about 3mm (⅛in).

3 Working on the back of the red card square, apply glue stick round the aperture, taking care not to get glue on the cut edges. Lay the black linen over it and stretch it over the aperture by passing a plastic ruler across the fabric.

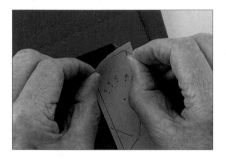

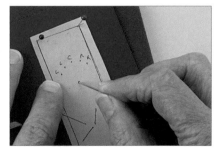

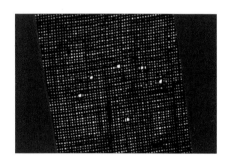

4 Place the card face up on the foam mat and use glass-headed pins to fix the template over the aperture.

5 Now use a size 18 chenille needle to prick through the dots on the template.

The holes made in the linen by the needle in step 5 are clearly visible. It is not necessary to mark them with chalk as this is such a small project.

6 Thread the 7mm (¼in) pink ribbon on the needle, then, working on the right side, take the tail end down through hole 1 in the fabric.

7 Always anchor ribbon on the wrong side behind the stitch to be worked, and when finishing off. Apply a little glue stick to the back of the fabric and use a glass-headed pin to smooth down the tail end of ribbon to secure it.

Tip
Using the eye end of another needle, stroke the underside of the ribbon to straighten and position it before stitching.

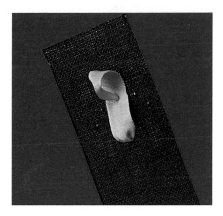

8   Turn the card face up, lay the ribbon (with a slight lift) over hole 2, then take the needle and ribbon down through the centre of the ribbon and hole 2.

9   Start to pull the ribbon carefully through itself and the fabric...

10   ...until the petal is formed. Do not pull it too tight or the shape will be lost. This is centre ribbon stitch.

Tip

To shape the petals, use the eye of a second needle the same size as the one used to embroider the ribbon.

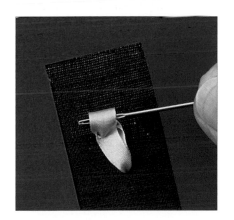

11   Bring the ribbon up carefully at 1 and lay it over the first stitch but this time take the needle down through the left-hand edge of the ribbon at 3 and place the eye end of a second needle in the loop to pull the ribbon over. This is a left ribbon stitch.

12   Pull the ribbon firmly over this needle, keeping it in place. Bring the first needle up again at 1 then remove the second needle.

13   Repeat steps 11 and 12 for the third petal, but this time take the needle down through the right-hand edge of the ribbon at 4. This is a right ribbon stitch. Fasten off at the back with a touch of the glue stick as before.

15 Using two strands of green embroidery thread and a crewel size 8 needle, work a straight stitch stem, coming up at 1 and down at 7. Bring the thread up just to the right-hand side of the stem, 7mm (¼in) up from the bottom.

14 Anchor a length of 7mm (¼in) pale pink ribbon at 1, lay the ribbon over the left petal, then work a left ribbon stitch at 5 and a right ribbon stitch at 6. Fasten off as before.

Tip

Avoid bringing the needle up through ribbon on the back of the work, as it will destroy the stitches previously worked.

16 Take the thread over then under the stem and back down the same hole to make a loop. Now bring the needle back up through the loop.

17 Pull the stitch tight to create a thorn and a kink in the stem, then take the needle down to make a tiny chain stitch and complete the stitch.

18 Next work a short straight stitch to create a leaf spur, then add two more thorns up the stem.

19 Using 4mm (¹⁄₈in) deep moss ribbon, work a left, right and centre ribbon stitch to form the calyx. Anchor the 7mm (¹⁄₄in) deep moss ribbon at 8 and work three centre ribbon stitches to form the leaves. Work the middle leaf through the card as shown.

20 Use a mapping pin to make two holes in the card 15mm (⁵⁄₈in) from the left-hand side, 6mm (⁷⁄₁₆in) down from the top and up from the bottom. Use the 4mm (¹⁄₈in) pale pink ribbon to lay in a straight stitch, anchoring each end on the back of the card with a touch of glue stick.

21 Tie a bow with the rest of the 4mm (¹⁄₈in) pale pink ribbon, then use a single strand of pink thread to anchor the bow through the ribbon and the card.

Tip
It is easier to position a bow with streamers if it is tied separately and then anchored with a thread.

Tip
The piece of card fixed behind the aperture takes up the tension of the fabric and should be added to all cards with fabric in an aperture.

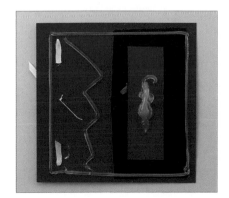

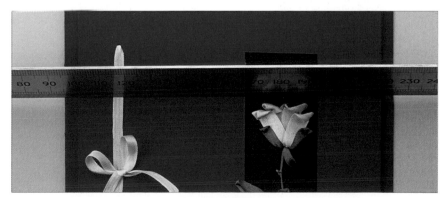

22 Glue the small piece of red card from step 2 on the back of the embroidery, then apply strips of silicone sealant as shown.

23 Place the embroidered panel neatly in the centre of the folded card blank, then use a ruler to level the card on the sealant. The sealant will ensure that the panel sticks firmly to the card but is slightly raised from it.

FUCHSIAS

Silk ribbon gathered with a row of tiny running stitches is used to create these fuchsias. The flowers will vary depending on the width of ribbon used, the length gathered and the colour. You can transform the fuchsias by using a little paint.

YOU WILL NEED

Single-fold white card blank, 10.5 x 15cm (4$\frac{1}{8}$ x 6in)

White card, 8.5 x 12cm (3$\frac{1}{4}$ x 4$\frac{3}{4}$in)

White fabric, 8cm (3$\frac{1}{8}$in) square

Glass-headed pin, mapping pin and foam mat

Craft knife and cutting mat

Glue stick

Silk paints: red, magenta and yellow

Paintbrushes, tile, kitchen sponge and an iron

Needles: a size 13 (extra large) and two size 18 (medium) chenille and a crewel size 8

13mm ($\frac{1}{2}$in) silk ribbon: 50cm (20in) of pale pink (05)

7mm ($\frac{1}{4}$in) silk ribbon: 50cm (20in) of dusky red (114) 25cm (10in) of deep green (21)

4mm ($\frac{1}{8}$in) silk ribbon: 50cm (20in) of dusky red (114) 25cm (10in) of deep green (21)

Toning stranded embroidery thread and green coton à broder

Scissors and tweezers

Clear silicone sealant

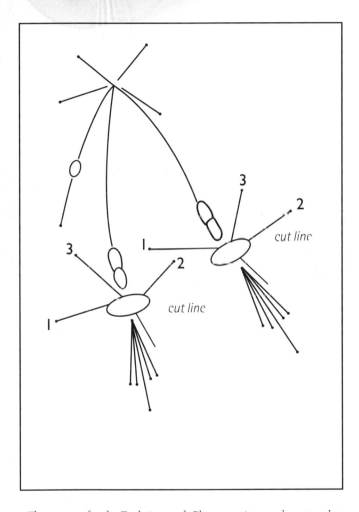

The pattern for the Fuchsias card. Photocopy it to make a template.

Tip

Gathered flowers are worked using short lengths of ribbon – a perfect way to use up your odds and ends. Always use a toning thread to gather ribbon.

1   Use the template, a glass-headed pin, a mapping pin and a foam mat to transfer the design on to the piece of white card.

2   Use the craft knife to cut round the oval shapes where the flower petals will sit.

3   Use a glue stick to stick the white fabric on the back of the card.

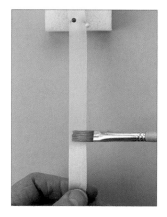

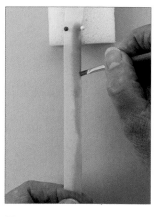

4   Mix the red, magenta and yellow silk paints on the tile to create the colour for the fuchsia.

5   Pin one end of the 13mm (½in) pale pink ribbon to the kitchen sponge, then use a paintbrush to wet the ribbon.

6   Use a small brush to apply colour to one side of the ribbon. Note how it spreads across the ribbon.

7   Add more colour down the selvedge of the ribbon and hang it up to dry. Iron the ribbon to set the silk paint.

Tip

Silk dries very quickly, but if you wish to speed up the process, a hairdryer is useful. It will also stop paint from spreading too far if too much has been used on either ribbon or fabric.

8   Knot the end of a strand of toning thread and take it through one end of the painted ribbon, 1cm (³/₈in) from the tail end, on the pale edge. Make a stitch over the edge to anchor the thread to the selvedge.

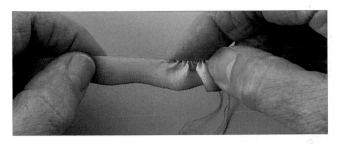

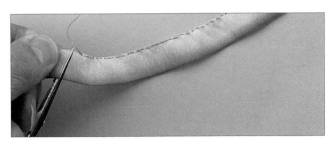

9 Start to work tiny running stitches along the selvedge.

10 Work a 10cm (4in) length of running stitch, then trim the ribbon diagonally 1cm (³/₈in) from the last stitch. Do not cut the thread.

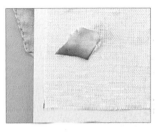

11 Use a craft knife and cutting mat to cut a slot through the card and fabric below each oval.

12 Use the flat end of a pair of tweezers to push the knotted end of the ribbon through the slot in the right-hand flower, with the stitched edge nearest the centre.

13 On the back of the panel, adjust the angle of the ribbon in the slot so that it is parallel to the cut end. Secure the tail with glue.

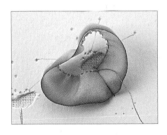

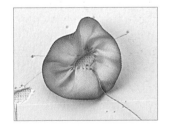

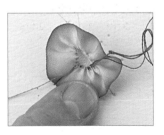

14 Pull the running stitch thread slightly to start the gather, then repeat steps 12 and 13 to secure the other end of the ribbon. The running stitch thread must stay on top.

15 Place a finger in the centre of the loop of ribbon, then gently pull the running stitch to gather the selvedge.

16 Keep checking the size of the gathered loop until it fits the edge of the cutout oval shape.

17 Using a toning thread, work in stab stitch along the gathered edge from the knotted end around to the right-hand end of the oval, tight to the card.

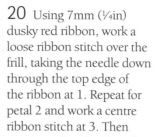

18 Fold the top of the gathered ribbon down, then stab stitch the selvedge, tight to the card, across the top of the oval.

19 Open up the gathered ribbon and stab stitch the left-hand side of the bottom of the oval. Take the working thread and the gathering stitch thread to the back of the panel and tie off both.

20 Using 7mm (¼in) dusky red ribbon, work a loose ribbon stitch over the frill, taking the needle down through the top edge of the ribbon at 1. Repeat for petal 2 and work a centre ribbon stitch at 3. Then use 4mm (⅛in) ribbon the same colour to work the straight stitch tube. Add a tiny 4mm (⅛in) deep green stitch at the top. Use pink and white embroidery thread to work straight stitches with French knots at the ends to form the stamens.

21 Work the second flower in the same way, then add a straight stitch bud. The stems are coton à broder straight stitches and the leaves are ribbon stitch using 7mm (¼in) deep green ribbon.

The finished card (page 120)

I attached the panel to the folded card blank using clear silicone sealant as described on page 119. When it was dry, I used a 4mm (⅛in) dusky red ribbon to highlight the design, using the following method. Use a mapping pin to make holes in three corners of the card front and in the bow position as shown. Tie a small looped bow in the centre of the ribbon and pull the knot tight. Leaving a long end at the back, anchor the bow in position with a stitch in a toning thread, then use this thread to work a stitch to anchor the ribbon at the corner. Now tie off the ends to secure them. Keep the ribbon flat on the front and, referring to page 116 steps 6 and 7, anchor the ends on the back of the card.

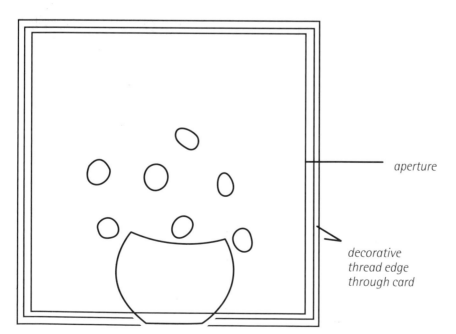

aperture

decorative
thread edge
through card

The template for the Bowl of Anemones card on page 127, shown full size.

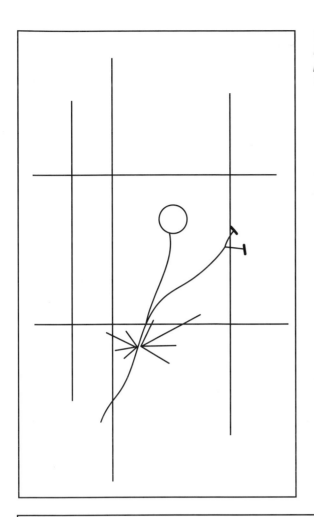

The template for the Buttercup card on page 127, shown full size.

The template for the Poppies card on page 127, shown full size.

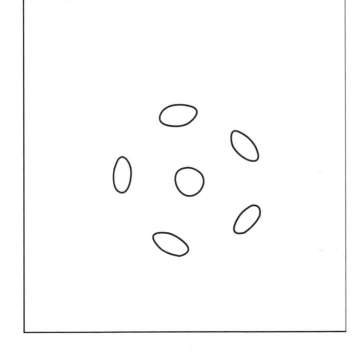

The template for the Scabious Garland card on page 127, shown full size. You do not need a template for the left-hand panel.

Poppies

Using red (02) 7mm (¼in) ribbon, gather four 6cm (2¼in) lengths, plus a 1cm (³/₈in) tail at each end. Now proceed as in steps 8–16, but use a chenille size 18 needle to take the ribbon through the card. Gather the ribbon evenly round the aperture, stab stitch it in place and using two black threads, fill the centres with two-loop French knots. Work straight stitch buds with 7mm (¼in) moss green (20) ribbon and add a straight stitch stem, couching through the card with a toning thread to curve it. Use this thread to work the fly stitch leaves.

Bowl of Anemones

Glue pale green fabric in the aperture, cut out the bowl shape and position it. Work the flowers as for the poppies using 7mm (¼in) ribbon in deep pink (128), delph blue (117), deep red (49) and purple (177), then work two-loop French knots in black to fill the centres. Using green coton à broder, work tiny fan shapes for the leaves. Edge the card with two-coloured threads.

Buttercup

Cut a piece of black linen on the straight of the grain, fringe each side and press. Make holes for flowers in a piece of card and stick it behind the fabric but not the fringe, and make holes for flowers. Work the flower and bud (two stitches) as for the poppies with 7mm (¼in) yellow (15) ribbon, then work a series of loops for the stamens, anchor off, then cut the loops. Couch the two thread lines in position and work the two straight stitches with 2mm (¹/₁₆ in) moss green ribbon. Work the stem and add leaves using 2mm (¹/₁₆in) green ribbon.

Scabious Garland

Prepare both white panels as in steps 2 and 3. Mix blue silk paint with a hint of magenta to shade 66cm (26in) of 7mm (¼in) white (03) ribbon patchily. Dry then press the ribbon. Work as for the poppies but gather seven 6cm (2¼in) lengths plus 1cm (³/₈in) tails and use a strand each of pale green and yellow for the centres.

Tip

To make an edging as in the Bowl of Anemones card: make a pinhole at each corner of the card, thread a needle with a coloured thread and take it down through a hole, leaving half of the thread at the front. Lay the top thread over the next hole and bring the needle up, over and back down to hold this thread. Keeping the top thread taut, work the next two corners, unthread the needle and use it to take the top thread down at the start. Tie the ends off securely. Repeat with a second colour.

Index